EXPLORING CAREERS

Careers in Environmental Conservation

Christine Wilcox

ReferencePoint Press®

© 2018 ReferencePoint Press, Inc.
Printed in the United States

For more information, contact:
ReferencePoint Press, Inc.
PO Box 27779
San Diego, CA 92198
www.ReferencePointPress.com

LIBRARY OF CONGRESS CATALOGING-IN-PUBLICATION DATA

Name: Wilcox, Christine, author.
Title: Careers in Environmental Conservation/by Christine Wilcox.
Description: San Diego, CA: ReferencePoint Press, Inc., 2018. | Series: Exploring Careers | Includes bibliographical references and index. | Audience: Grade 9 to 12.
Identifiers: LCCN 2016046468 (print) | LCCN 2017005618 (ebook) | ISBN 9781682822036 (hardback) | ISBN 9781682822043 (eBook)
Subjects: LCSH: Environmentalism—Vocational guidance—Juvenile literature. | Vocational guidance—Juvenile literature.
Classification: LCC GE115 .W548 2018 (print) | LCC GE115 (ebook) | DDC 333.72023--dc23
LC record available at https://lccn.loc.gov/2016046468

Contents

Saving the Earth for a Living

What Is Environmental Conservation?

Environmental conservation is a broad field that encompasses any profession that helps make life on earth sustainable. Sustainability is an important concern because humans are using up the planet's resources at an alarming rate. The outcome of centuries of industrialization and development are more keenly being noticed and felt: Fossil fuels are being depleted, the world's forests are being cut down, and pollution is contaminating the air and the oceans. Scientists now agree that all of this activity—and most prominently, the burning of fossil fuels—is causing the earth's climate to warm at an unprecedented rate; and future generations may be left with a world devastated by extreme weather, mass extinctions, and rising sea levels. Whole species and ecosystems are disappearing before scientists can understand how they work or how they affect humanity. Environmental scientists warn that if there ever was a time to conserve and sustain the planet's resources, that time is now.

A Wealth of Opportunities

In response to this crisis, more and more jobs are being created in conservation and sustainability than ever before. According to new data from the labor market analysis firm Economic Modeling Specialists International, US employment relating to conservation, the environment, and wildlife preservation will increase by 19 percent from 2016 to 2021. That rise makes conservation the eighth-fastest-growing industry in the country. These are not low-paying jobs planting trees or passing out flyers; sustainability and conservation are a

4

multibillion-dollar industry. For instance, the Nature Conservancy, a nonprofit environmental organization involved in scientific research, conservation, and political advocacy, had assets totaling nearly $7 billion in 2015. Organizations like these need all sorts of skill sets to run efficiently: financial planners, marketing experts, scientists, teachers and educators, lawyers, and high-level program managers.

Environmentalism has become part of everyday conversations. "Green" and "sustainable" products on store shelves attract customers. Politicians have made conservation part of the national debate, attracting more attention to the field and the need for a specialized workforce. The Obama administration made green energy a national priority, expanding opportunities for engineers, scientists, and inventors working on the problem of supplying the world with energy without burning fossil fuels. And businesses are reforming their practices in droves to reduce the negative impact they have on the environment. More and more businesses are creating new positions in sustainability and are looking for talented people to help them conserve precious natural resources, reduce pollution, and educate members of the public about issues they care about. In fact, environmental education has become an important part of the curriculum in many school districts, and teachers can now combine their passion for conservation with their love of teaching to help create the next generation of environmental leaders.

Preparing for a Green Career

Because opportunities are expanding, experts encourage students who are thinking about a career in environmental conservation to learn as much as possible about the duties and functions of these jobs. Educating oneself is the best way to find out what career options are available and what type of job is the best fit. Preparation and investigation are important, said Emily Chan, a corporate sustainability consultant, in a February 2014 article posted on the career website the Muse. "Slow down," Chan wrote. "Before you can really decide what you want to devote your time (and money) to, you need to get your hands dirty and learn what you actually like." She suggests that students volunteer as much as they can in high school and college and then work in the field for a while before settling on a career path.

Careers in Environmental Conservation

Occupation	Entry-Level Education	2015 Median Pay
Animal care and service worker	High school dipoloma or equivalent	$21,260
Atmospheric scientist, including meteorologist	Bachelor's degree	$89,820
Environmental engineering technician	Associate's degree	$48,650
Environmental science and protection technician	Associate's degree	$43,030
Environmental scientist and specialist	Bachelor's degree	$67,460
Forest and conservation worker	High school dipoloma or equivalent	$26,190
Hazardous materials removal worker	High school dipoloma or equivalent	$39,690
Hydrologist	Bachelor's degree	$79,550
Solar photovoltaic installer	High school dipoloma or equivalent	$37,830
Urban and regional planner	Master's degree	$68,220
Veterinarian	Doctoral or professional degree	$88,490
Water and wastewater treatment plant and systems operator	High school dipoloma or equivalent	$44,790
Zoologist and wildlife biologist	Bachelor's degree	$59,680

Source: Bureau of Labor Statistics, *Occupational Outlook Handbook*. www.bls.gov/ooh.

To prepare students for this growing field, colleges and universities all over the country now offer degree programs in environmental science and environmental studies. These degrees expose students to multiple disciplines, and they can lead to careers in all but the most specialized jobs in environmental conservation. Careers in science have the most earning potential, but there are good opportunities in business management and education as well. Students who prefer hands-on work to academic or theoretical activities can attend a two-year technician training program in areas such as environmental science, forestry, environmental engineering, or wildlife veterinary medicine. Technicians make good incomes, and credits earned at technician training programs usually can be transferred to four-year college programs if students wish to advance in their fields. Thus, technicians who want to become scientists already have experience and training in their field of choice and can easily move along the new career path.

Career Satisfaction

Perhaps the best reason to choose a career in environmental conservation is personal satisfaction. "Quite simply these professionals say that the jobs they do are rewarding," said Tim Balcon, chief executive of the Institute of Environmental Management and Assessment. As he explained to James Murray in an April 2016 article published in the online news magazine *Business Green*, "There is a real sense of doing something ethical and positive with their careers. . . . Plus salaries are on the rise and employer support for professional development is high. All of that adds up to satisfied workers who really bring their best to work." Indeed, according to a 2016 worldwide survey, 82 percent of sustainability professionals say that they are satisfied with their careers.

With rising salaries, expanding opportunities, and the personal reward of knowing that one's job makes a difference, there has never been a better time to choose a career in environmental conservation. Students who follow this path today will shape the environment of tomorrow, building a sustainable future and ensuring that life will thrive on this planet for millennia to come.

Environmental Educator

At a Glance
Environmental Educator

Minimum Educational Requirements
High school diploma or equivalent

Personal Qualities
Excellent communication and presentation skills; creativity

Certification and Licensing
Required to teach K–12 in schools

Working Conditions
Indoor and outdoor classrooms, some travel

Salary Range
As of May 2015, $36,190 to $85,550 full time; $9 to $12 per hour part time

Employers
Schools, nonprofits, government, private companies

Future Job Outlook
Growth of 6 percent through 2024

In this time of uncertainty about the future of the earth's environment, educating young people about environmental issues is one of the most important goals of conservationists. Environmental educators are at the forefront of this effort, which aims to create a new generation of environmentally conscious individuals who have both the knowledge and the will to confront pressing issues like global warming, resource sustainability, and species extinction. This exciting career path allows educators to combine their love of teaching with their passion for conservation.

Environmental educators are usually licensed teachers or professional trainers with experience in instructional design and learning theory. They work with schools, government education programs, or institutions like zoos and nature reserves to

8

develop and design comprehensive educational programs. Environmental educators create education programs, develop course content and presentation material, and handle presentation scheduling and other logistics. They are usually involved in marketing their programs, and many are also involved in fund-raising, budgeting, and program management.

Some environmental educators work directly for conservation centers and educate the public about a single issue. For instance, environmental educators at the Wolf Conservation Center of New York incorporate wolves into their on- and off-site presentations, run the center's Wolf Camp for Kids, and develop curriculum for teachers. Other environmental educators work for schools or school districts and teach students about a wide variety of conservation issues. One such educator is Andra Yeghoian, the director of sustainability at Bishop O'Dowd High School in Oakland, California. Yeghoian runs the school's Center for Environmental Studies (CES) and works with teachers to develop courses, programs, and extracurricular activities. For instance, Yeghoian has created programs in which students manage the CES building's 4-acre (1.6-ha) "Living Lab" greenhouse and compost system as part of their classwork, participate in school-wide recycling and sustainability programs, and even travel to places like Yellowstone National Park and Costa Rica to work with ecologists who are doing research in conservation issues. "This is my dream job," Yeghoian said in an August 2013 article on the Bishop O'Dowd High School web page. "Our graduates will understand . . . sustainability and incorporate it in their decision-making." Because of Yeghoian's work, Bishop O'Dowd High School was named a 2016 US Department of Education Green Ribbon School, an award that recognizes schools that promote sustainability and environmental education.

Not all environmental educators are education professionals, however. Some are college students, retirees, or just people who happen to have specialized knowledge—or a keen interest—in environmental issues. These people work as presenters at zoos, nature centers, or other nonprofits that educate the public about conservation. Presenter jobs tend to be part time and pay a low hourly rate, and many are volunteer positions. Other people design and deliver educational presentations as part of a related job. For instance, animal keepers or trainers are often the ones who present a zoo's animal show, and park rangers regularly give presentations about environmental issues, such as the effects of pollution on forest ecosystems. And some environmental educators have job titles like director of communication or public relations associate for nonprofits. In short, anyone involved in the field of conservation can get involved in environmental education.

How Do You Become an Environmental Educator?

Education

While it is not absolutely necessary to have a college degree to secure a job as an environmental educator, most have at least a bachelor's degree. Some study education and secure a teaching license so they can work in schools, while others get degrees in ecology or another conservation-related science. A popular major in this field is environmental studies. This is an interdisciplinary program that draws from many different fields such as geology, biology, public policy, and law. "You can expect to study many disciplines from the natural sciences to the social sciences to humanities, with the focus on learning to make educated judgments about environmental issues through careful, objective analysis," wrote Carol Ruhl in a March 2015 article posted on Enviro Education's website, where she works as an environmental education specialist. "There is also often great latitude for students to create their own curriculum and emphasis within the major." Ruhl also suggests students interested in environmental education pursue an internship to show prospective employers that they can succeed in the workplace.

Experts also suggest that students seek out opportunities in college to develop their communication skills. "One [way to get ahead] is to have great communication skills—oral and written communication," said John Callewaert, director of the Institute for Community and Environment at Colby-Sawyer College. As he explained in Ruhl's 2015 article, "Students need to push themselves to get this. The more confidence one can build the more interested potential employers will be. Students should try to take advantage of as many public speaking experiences as they can."

Many agencies and environmental groups also offer certificate programs in environmental education. These programs are aimed at teachers interested in transitioning to careers in environmental education or in incorporating conservation subjects into their curriculums. A certificate from a reputable agency can give students a competitive edge in the job market while teaching them valuable skills in how to engage students and design programs.

Volunteer Work and Internships

Volunteering is an excellent way for students to gain experience and improve their job prospects. Many nonprofits have environmental education programs that use volunteers, and high school and college students can either assist the presenter or develop their own presentations. Students can offer to host an educational activity or give a short presentation at a day camp or to a scouting troop. Learning to teach others takes practice, and these types of volunteer opportunities will build teaching and presentation skills.

Students can also volunteer in other ways at centers that address environmental issues they care about. Environmental educators need to understand the material they are teaching, and working directly with conservationists is an excellent way to learn. It also shows prospective employers a passion for and commitment to environmental issues—key characteristics of effective educators.

Skills and Personality

Teachers—especially those who teach young people—tend to be extroverted and outgoing individuals. The best environmental educators are great teachers, and they use these personality traits to engage and excite their audiences. As public speakers, they must be confident in front of a crowd and have excellent communication skills. And because they often teach both children and adults, they must be able to engage people of all ages.

Usually, environmental educators design their own programs. To do this effectively, they must have a firm grasp of learning theory and be familiar with various presentation methods and technologies. They must also be creative, and those who create programs from scratch must have basic artistic or graphic design skills.

Environmental educators who design or manage large programs must have administrative and management skills. They often need to manage a staff of employees or volunteers, meet with stakeholders, apply for grants, manage budgets, and plan large events.

Finally, all environmental educators have a deep love for nature and a desire to protect it. They also need specialized knowledge about the topics they teach, which many gain through volunteer work on conservation projects in their spare time. They are passionate people who view their career as a way to make a difference in the fate of the planet.

On the Job

Employers

Just about any organization that is concerned with educating the public about conservation issues can employ environmental educators. Educators work in schools, zoos and aquariums, nature centers, nonprofits, and summer camps and recreation centers. Many educators are employed by the federal and state and local governments. For instance, the Environmental Protection Agency's Office of Environmental Education employs educators to run programs that promote environmental education throughout the United States. And North Carolina's Office of Environmental Education hires environmental educators to staff its Environmental Educator Certification Program. There are also government jobs available in museums like the Smithsonian in Washington, DC, and in national and state parks.

Finally, many private companies have created new positions in sustainability. Environmental educators often staff these positions and educate consumers—usually through marketing and social media—about the ways in which a company works to reduce its global footprint. More and more companies are creating these positions in response to the public's concern about conservation issues.

Working Conditions

Most environmental educators spend at least some of their time in nature. Conservation centers often conduct their programs and classes outdoors, and some environmental educators work at summer camps or outdoor programs for young people.

For the rest of the time, educators usually work in an office or classroom setting. Many travel frequently for their jobs and teach classes at local schools or community centers. They tend to be on their feet for most of the day and often have to set up and break down their equipment, so a degree of physical fitness is required.

Most educators work regular hours, but those who teach outside of a school setting may work evenings and weekends, and some run overnight summer programs.

Earnings

The Bureau of Labor Statistics (BLS) does not collect employment information for environmental educators. The website Environmental Science groups environmental educators with elementary school teachers. As of May 2015 the BLS states that elementary school teacher salaries range from about $36,190 to $85,550 per year, depending upon responsibilities, experience, and seniority. A part-time environmental educator or an educator with only a high school diploma can expect to make about $9 to $12 per hour.

Opportunities for Advancement

There are many ways to advance one's career in environmental education. Educators can design their own career paths depending upon their interests. Those in top jobs develop entire curriculums for school districts, direct programs within government agencies, and run the education programs for large zoos and aquariums. It is an exciting field with a wealth of opportunities available for individuals committed to improving their skills.

To secure higher-paying jobs with more responsibility, environmental educators should gain experience in curriculum development and program management and administration. They should also become experts in the conservation issues they teach. Becoming certified in environmental education and getting a teaching certificate can also lead to better jobs with more responsibility.

What Is the Future Outlook for Environmental Educators?

While the BLS does not track job trends for this career, it does project that employment of K–12 teachers will grow at an average rate of 6 percent from 2014 to 2024. Experts confirm that opportunities for environmental educators are expected to increase in future years. Monster.com notes that more jobs are being created in response to the public's growing concern about environmental issues. Many schools and state and local governments have created departments of conservation, and sustainability positions are being created in private businesses that have a potential impact on the environment (such as oil companies). These trends indicate that job prospects for environmental educators will increase in the years to come.

Find Out More

Environmental Protection Agency (EPA)
Office of Environmental Education
1200 Pennsylvania Ave. NW
Washington, DC 20460
website: www.epa.gov/education

The EPA's Office of Environmental Education website is a clearinghouse of information about environmental education. It includes resources and publications, information for educators, and links to environmental education resources.

National Environmental Education and Training Foundation (NEEF)
4301 Connecticut Ave. NW, Suite 160
Washington, DC 20008
website: www.neefusa.org

The NEEF is an independent nonprofit organization that works with the EPA to educate the public about the environment and conservation. Its website contains a wealth of conservation information aimed at teachers, as well as information about grants for students pursuing a career in conservation.

North American Association for Environmental Education (NAAEE)
2000 P St. NW, Suite 540
Washington, DC 20036
website: https://naaee.org

The NAAEE is dedicated to promoting excellence in environmental education. Its website describes its many education initiatives and includes information about careers. There are also articles and blog posts by professional educators working in environmental education.

Steinhardt Environmental Conservation Education Program
New York University
82 Washington Square E
New York, NY 10003
website: http://steinhardt.nyu.edu/teachlearn/environmental

New York University has one of the top graduate programs in environmental education in the country. Its website contains information, research, and news in environmental education, as well as interviews with recent graduates working in the field.

Environmental Technician

What Does an Environmental Technician Do?

In 2011, when South Carolina decided to deepen the shipping lanes at the Port of Charleston, engineers had to figure out what to do with the millions of cubic yards of sediment that would be dredged up from the bottom of the Charleston Harbor. Could it be placed safely in a disposal site, or would it be toxic and need special treatment and handling? Or could it be used to shore up the coastline or create new habitats for wildlife? To answer these questions, environmental technicians took core samples at more than a hundred sites at the bottom of the harbor, working from boats outfitted with specialized drilling equipment. The work was not easy; the boats were positioned in the shipping lane, and a storm system made the tides higher and the currents stronger. But these highly skilled professionals took hundreds of samples, analyzed them, and gave the engineers in charge of the project a complete picture of the physical, chemical, and toxicological composition of the sediment. Because of their efforts, sediment from the dredging project, which will be completed in 2020, is being disposed of in a safe and environmentally friendly manner.

Environmental technicians are the unsung heroes of conservation and pollution control. By monitoring and testing the environment, these professionals help humans reduce their impact on the planet—and identify the polluters who flout the law. They sample air, water, and soil quality; they identify contaminants and gauge the health of local ecosystems; and they make sure large-scale projects like the deepening of the Charleston Harbor do not inadvertently destroy the environment—or endanger human health.

Environmental technicians who work in the field of environmental science do so under several different job titles, including environmental health and protection technician, laboratory technician, or laboratory specialist. (The janitorial industry also uses the job title "environmental technician," but these jobs are not related to environmental conservation.) Regardless of the title, these technicians are experts at sample collection and analysis. They gather organic and inorganic matter using specialized sampling equipment, which they calibrate and maintain. They test those samples in the laboratory for pollutants or evidence of an unhealthy ecosystem. Some test indoor environments for dangerous substances like radon. Some specialize in outdoor work, testing wilderness areas for pollutants. Some work with engineers or urban planners on new construction projects, while others work for government agencies, testing emissions or wastewater from manufacturing plants. More experienced technicians may develop innovative testing procedures or work directly with businesses to help them reduce their impact on the environment.

Becoming an environmental technician is an excellent career path for students who love the technical side of science but who may not want to pursue a four-year degree. Typically, new graduates can find jobs after only two years of training. In addition, students who follow this career path can later become environmental scientists (who often direct the work of environmental technicians). Those who choose to do this can usually transfer their academic credits from their environmental technician training program.

This exciting career has great potential for growth. As concern for the environment increases, more trained technicians will be needed to help enforce new environmental laws and regulations. It is a perfect career choice for technically inclined students who want to protect the environment from the dangers of contaminants and pollutants.

How Do You Become an Environmental Technician?

Education

Formal training is almost always required to work as an environmental technician. Training programs can be found at community colleges, technical schools, or within the environmental studies schools of some colleges and universities. Programs teach the way ecosystems work and cover aspects of chemistry, physics, and mathematics as they relate to sampling and laboratory work. These programs are heavy on practical training and teach students how to use and maintain equipment, how to run tests in the lab, and how to interpret test results.

Environmental technician programs tend to be very popular with students who enjoy the hands-on nature of the training. For instance, students in the environmental technician program at Fleming College in Ontario, Canada, love that they spend so much time outdoors, learning about the environment firsthand. Students train with the same field equipment they will later use on the job, which makes them more likely to find employment after graduation. And for part of the program, they work in a wilderness setting, collecting samples and processing them in the lab. As one student explained in an April 2015 video Fleming College posted on YouTube, these programs "make your learning tangible. . . . You really do get the larger picture of what a lot of these ecosystems are."

Most environmental technician programs are two years long and award associate's degrees. There are also shorter programs available that offer more concentrated training in sampling and lab techniques to people who have a background in environmental science, who are already working in laboratories, or who have already earned a bachelor's degree. Finally, some state-run programs award licenses that allow environmental technicians to get jobs as state inspectors, professionals who certify that structures or job sites do not contain any environmental hazards.

Volunteer Work and Internships

Virtually any volunteer experience relating to environmental science is pertinent to this career. The most useful volunteer opportunities involve surveying or sampling the environment or working with laboratory equipment. For instance, some local governments monitor the health of their local ecosystems and occasionally need volunteers to collect samples. Others have environmental educational programs that involve some volunteering. Science clubs are also a great way to get experience with lab equipment, and some clubs volunteer to work with scientists on research projects.

Internships or cooperative education programs are also available for high school and college students in labs or with conservation projects. These programs not only give students experience in the field, but they can also make it easier for new graduates to get their first job. Volunteer work and internships help new graduates stand out from other applicants. They also demonstrate a commitment to environmental welfare.

Skills and Personality

Environmental technicians need to be very methodical and detail oriented. Samples must be gathered and tested in the same way, procedures must be followed to avoid contamination, and equipment must be properly calibrated and maintained. For this reason, the most successful people in this field have a natural aversion to sloppy work. They get satisfaction from following procedures to the letter, and they take pride in producing reliable results.

In addition, environmental technicians must be able to follow directions, communicate effectively (orally and in writing), and work well in a team environment. And perhaps most importantly, they need strong critical-thinking skills. Experienced environmental technicians synthesize large amounts of data to reach conclusions about environmental hazards, and they sometimes make recommendations about how to alleviate them. This takes a combination of experience, sound reasoning, and good judgment.

On the Job

Employers

Most environmental technicians work for environmental consulting firms or for the government. Governments hire technicians to make sure the environment is safe, to identify polluters, and to help with remediating—or cleaning up—toxic environments. Environmental consulting firms hire technicians to help their clients comply with local, state, and federal laws. Some experienced environmental technicians are independent consultants or work directly for large corporations, such as oil or pharmaceutical companies. Environmental technicians who prefer working in the lab can find employment with testing laboratories. Finally, technicians who are interested in environmental science can work on research projects that involve sampling and data collection.

Earnings

According to the Bureau of Labor Statistics (BLS), the median salary for an environmental technician in 2015 was $43,030 per year, with a salary range of about $26,890 to $71,860. Environmental technicians who worked for local government agencies made the most, with a median salary of $45,720. Those who worked for testing laboratories made the least, with a median salary of $37,010. The website PayScale notes that in 2016 the average wage for an environmental technician was $15.52 per hour. Some employers pay overtime, which is typically 50 percent more than a worker's hourly rate.

According to the news magazine *U.S. News & World Report*, some locations pay environmental technicians more than others. For instance, environmental technicians made the highest salaries in Las Vegas, Nevada, where the average salary in 2015 was $69,240.

Working Conditions

Environmental technicians can work indoors or outdoors, though most work in both environments. Those who specialize in lab work spend a lot of time in the laboratory running tests. Those who specialize in field collection spend time in a wide variety of environments, many of which are hazardous. For instance, some technicians spend days in the wilderness, wading through streams or hiking over rough terrain. Others take samples at hazardous waste sites or inside contaminated buildings.

Technicians are often required to travel to job sites and may have to work irregular hours. Work can be seasonal, especially if they are testing in outdoor environments. Sampling work can also be physically demanding. Some environmental technicians spend most of their workdays on their feet, carrying heavy equipment or crouching and bending. For this reason, good physical fitness is usually required.

Opportunities for Advancement

Early in their careers, most environmental technicians work under close supervision. As they gain experience, they can move into supervisory or management positions, and can eventually manage large or specialized projects. Some job titles for advanced positions are environmental project manager and environmental specialist.

Environmental technicians who want to advance further will need to get a bachelor's degree in environmental science, chemistry, or a related scientific major. Some environmental technicians go on to become environmental scientists—scientists who analyze environmental problems and develop solutions. Others specialize in conservation work with nonprofits or teach in environmental technician programs.

What Is the Future Outlook for Environmental Technicians?

According to the BLS, employment of environmental technicians is projected to grow at a faster-than-average rate of 9 percent from 2014 to 2024. Concerns about the environment are on the rise—especially as new technologies are developed that could adversely impact human health and the environment. Governments are responding to these concerns by researching the effects of human activity on the environment and passing new laws to protect it. Because environmental technicians are needed for both research and monitoring, the BLS expects governments to create more of these positions in coming years.

Corporations are also becoming increasingly concerned about their impact on the environment, and many seek to develop cleaner and greener ways to do business. To do this, most hire environmental consulting companies, which employ more than a quarter of the environmental technicians working in the United States. Corporations and nonprofits are also sponsoring more research projects in sustainability and conservation—projects that need the services of environmental technicians. Finally, the BLS projects that many new job opportunities will open up in this field in the coming decade due to retirement or other forms of attrition. Experts agree that the outlook for this career is promising for the foreseeable future.

Find Out More

Association of Public Health Laboratories (APHL)
8515 Georgia Ave., Suite 700
Silver Spring, MD 20910
website: www.aphl.org

The APHL is a professional development and training organization for laboratory workers in the area of public health. Its website contains news articles related to current environmental health issues, as well as links to educational exercises and webinars.

Fleming College
School of Environmental & Natural Resource Sciences
599 Brealey Dr.
Peterborough, ON
K9J 7B1, Canada
website: https://flemingcollege.ca/school/environmental-and-natural-resource-sciences

The environmental technician program at Fleming College trains environmental technicians to work in the remote wilderness settings of Ontario,

Canada. Its website contains videos, articles, and general information about what it is like to be an environmental technician in Canada.

National Environmental Health Association (NEHA)
720 S. Colorado Blvd., Suite 1000-N
Denver, CO 80246
website: www.neha.org

The NEHA is a national professional society for environmental health technicians and other practitioners. Its website contains details about its licensing programs for environmental technicians as well as scholarship information.

St. Petersburg College
Environmental Science Technology Program
PO Box 13489
St. Petersburg, FL 33733
website: www.spcollege.edu

The environmental science technology program at St. Petersburg College has specializations in sustainability, water resource management, and environmental resources and energy management. Its website contains videos, sample curricula, and information about careers.

Forester

What Does a Forester Do?

Talis Kalnars is a forester in Great Britain known for developing innovative management techniques that boost the health of forests. Like other foresters, he uses scientific knowledge to try to understand the thousands of complex interactions that go on between forest species. But according to Kalnars, science has a long way to go. "Forestry is an art," he explained in a May 2014 article by Phil Morgan published on the website the Ecologist. "Of course the art has to be informed by science, but . . . how you manage a forest comes down to personal judgment." For instance, one of his ideas (which he notes has not yet been scientifically proven), is that birch trees somehow help other trees grow. "Where there is Birch there is more natural regeneration of other trees," he explained. "Maybe it's the dappled shade, or some chemical effect, or the mycorrhizal fungi around the roots. . . . You have to see the forest as a community, complete with community support."

Foresters study this community. They are conservation

At a Glance

Forester

Minimum Educational Requirements
Bachelor's degree

Personal Qualities
Strong critical-thinking, analysis, and communication skills

Certification and Licensing
Licensing is required in some states; certification is optional

Working Conditions
Offices, labs, and woodland settings

Salary Range
As of May 2015, about $38,660 to $84,980

Number of Jobs
About 8,590 as of 2015

Future Job Outlook
Growth of 7 percent through 2024

A New York forester examines bark from a damaged tree to determine the extent of southern pine beetle infestation. As conservation scientists, foresters study, analyze, and monitor the health of forest ecosystems.

scientists concerned with understanding one of the most complex ecosystems on the planet. They not only study how elements of a forest interact with each other but also how forests affect the health of the planet as a whole. They also work to make forests, which are important natural resources, sustainable over the long term. As the world's forests are threatened by climate change, fire, human encroachment, pollution, and clear-cutting, the job of foresters is becoming increasingly important.

Foresters who manage federal and state land study and monitor the health of the forest. They supervise surveying teams, improve the habitat for animals that are beneficial to the forest, remove certain plants (including trees) or supervise controlled burns to boost forest health, educate the public about the forest ecosystem, and try to reduce the harmful impact of human recreational activities. Foresters who work with logging companies or as timber consultants also manage the health of forests. They survey plant and animal life, identify trees that can be logged and supervise their removal, and oversee forest regeneration. There are also several forestry specialties. Procurement foresters facilitate the sale of timber. Urban foresters manage the trees and other plant life in cities and are concerned with the way urban forests can improve air quality and storm water runoff. And conservation education foresters educate the public about forest ecosystems and threats to those ecosystems.

Most experienced foresters are involved with planning and management tasks and scientific analysis rather than fieldwork (which is typically left to forest technicians and new forestry graduates). These foresters draw up plans to reduce the risk of wildfire, replenish growth, or combat damage caused by insects or invasive species. They analyze data gathered by surveyors to understand why one part of a forest is healthy and another is not. They also work closely with other agencies on larger ecological projects. For instance, many foresters believe that replenishing tropical forests will reduce the amount of carbon dioxide in the air and help slow global warming.

The field of forestry offers a multitude of opportunities for students who love the outdoors and want to understand and protect the nation's forests and the wild creatures that live there. These experts play a crucial role in environmental conservation and the health of the planet.

How Do You Become a Forester?

Education

Foresters need a bachelor's degree in forestry. Some jobs and certification programs require that applicants have graduated from a forestry program accredited by the Society of American Foresters (SAF), so students should go to an accredited program if possible. As of 2015, fifteen states also had a licensing or registration process in place for foresters. To use the title "professional forester" and practice forestry in these states, applicants usually must have a four-year degree in forestry and relevant work experience, and must pass an exam.

Foresters are scientists, and they are required to have an in-depth understanding of math and science. Students who attend an accredited program will study science, math, communication, computer science, and forestry subjects such as wetland analysis, water and soil quality, wildlife conservation, and environmental policy. Useful electives include courses in statistics, wildlife biology, and recreation management. Foresters also usually learn how to use technology involved in mapping and computer modeling. Those who are interested in doing forestry research or teaching should get at least a master's degree in forestry.

Some foresters start out as forestry workers or forestry technicians. Forestry workers do manual labor in forests, such as planting trees. Forestry technicians collect samples and do other surveying and management work under the supervision of a forester. Forestry technicians usually have completed a formal two-year training program that awards an associate's degree. Often, forestry technician program credits can be transferred to a four-year forestry program.

Volunteer Work and Internships

There are plenty of opportunities to do volunteer work in the nation's forests. Many forestry workers are volunteers; they build trails, plant trees, shore up erosion, and help maintain the health of the forest. Volunteers can also work with fire suppression teams, supervising controlled burns of parts of the forest to maintain forest health. They can also help with surveying, inventorying the types of trees and other plants that grow in the forest and noting damage done by insects. Paid summer internships are sometimes available for high school and college students who are interested in a career in forestry. Working as a volunteer can give students valuable experience in the wilderness—as well as give them an idea about whether a career in forestry is right for them.

Skills and Personality

Everything in a forest is interconnected, and many of those connections are not yet understood. Because a forester studies these connections, he or she is naturally curious and has strong critical-thinking skills. As scientists, foresters are analytical and methodical, taking the time to back up a hypothesis about an aspect of forest health or function with hard evidence. They also must have good communication skills to educate the public about the importance of forests.

Most people become foresters because they love forests and the outdoors, and many are avid hikers and campers. Because they do fieldwork (at least in the early part of their careers), foresters must have physical stamina and be physically fit. If they move into management positions, they will need to develop their project-planning and management skills.

All foresters are passionate about forest conservation. Even those who work for logging companies strive to ensure that logging practices are sustainable and important ecosystems are protected. More than anything else, this passion for one of the world's most mysterious and complex ecosystems is what defines a forester.

On the Job

Employers

State governments hire the most foresters—nearly three times as many as federal and local governments. In the western United States, foresters tend to work for the federal government because of the high concentration of national parks in that area. On the East Coast, foresters tend to work for the logging industry, for sawmills, or for private landowners. They can also work for scientists conducting research on the environment, for conservation organizations, or for colleges that have forestry programs.

Some foresters are private consultants. These professionals are hired by landowners or businesses to manage the health of forests on private land or to supervise timber harvesting. For instance, a construction company may hire a forester to estimate the value of the timber on a tract of land that it intends to clear and to supervise the removal of valuable trees.

Earnings

According to the Bureau of Labor Statistics (BLS), the median annual income of foresters was $58,230 in 2015, with a salary range of about $38,660 to $84,980. The timber industry and logging companies pay the highest salaries; foresters working for these companies earn about $64,000 a year on average. The federal government pays foresters an average salary of about $61,680. Foresters working in local and state government made the least, earning average salaries of $52,290 and $49,610, respectively.

Working Conditions

Many people assume that foresters spend all of their time in the woods, working alone for long stretches at a time. While many entry-level forestry jobs do require spending long periods of time working in the field, as a forester gains experience he or she will spend more and more time working in an office setting or in the laboratory. Foresters manage the health of the forest; and those management activities usually involve evaluating data, overseeing budgets, meeting with officials, and developing management plans—all work that occurs indoors.

In the field, foresters can work outdoors in all kinds of weather. They may need to walk long distances carrying heavy equipment over rough terrain, and may have to camp for days or weeks at a time while conducting surveys. Those who work with logging companies face multiple hazards—logging is a dangerous occupation, and people working near logging activities face threats from falling trees and branches, from heavy equipment, and from high levels of noise, which can damage hearing. Those who work as consultants may have to travel extensively, surveying forests over a wide area and supervising the work of forest technicians.

Opportunities for Advancement

As foresters gain experience, they usually advance to indoor management positions. One way to advance is to earn a master's degree in forestry or to take specialized postgraduate education courses. Working on research projects and publishing in academic and professional journals can also increase a forester's reputation and open up new employment opportunities.

Optional certification is also an important step to advancement. The SAF has a certification program for foresters who have graduated from accredited institutions. They must also have a certain amount of qualifying experience in the field and pass an exam.

What Is the Future Outlook for Foresters?

According to the BLS, foresters can expect a growth rate in employment of about 7 percent from 2014 to 2024, about as fast as average. Most of this employment growth will likely be in the western United States. In the West, the number of wildfires has been on the rise in recent years, which is especially problematic as more and more people are living closer to forests. Foresters will be needed to address these problems and come up with fire-management plans. In addition there has been an increased demand for timber, which means that foresters will be able to find more work for private companies.

Finally, as more ecological threats face the planet, sustaining and managing forests will become a priority. Forests are crucial to the world's ecosystems—they cool the planet, they create oxygen and clean the air, they host important animal species, and they provide us with fuel, building materials, paper, and other important natural resources. Specialized conservation scientists like foresters are needed to advance our understanding of how this complex and delicate ecosystem works and develop ways to sustain it. And the more that people understand the role of forests in keeping the planet healthy, the more resources they will invest in conserving them. For this reason, foresters will play a crucial role in environmental conservation for years to come.

Find Out More

Forest Stewards Guild
612 W. Main St., Suite 300
Madison, WI 53703
website: www.forestguild.org

The Forest Stewards Guild is a nonprofit organization made up of forestry professionals dedicated to restoring and sustaining the integrity of the planet's forests. Its website contains information about conservation programs, links to articles and publications, and a jobs section.

National Association of State Foresters (NASF)
444 N. Capitol St. NW, Suite 540
Washington, DC 20001
website: www.stateforesters.org

The NASF is a nonprofit professional organization for directors of state forestry agencies in the United States. Its website has links to forestry news, current issues in forestry and action plans, and a jobs board.

Society of American Foresters (SAF)
10100 Laureate Way
Bethesda, MD 20814
website: www.eforester.org

The SAF is a professional association that advances the practice of forestry and provides information and networking opportunities to foresters and natural resource professionals. Its website contains forestry news, information about advocacy and conservation, and a careers section.

US Forest Service
1400 Independence Ave. SW
Washington, DC 20250
website: www.fs.fed.us

The US Forest Service is the part of the US Department of Agriculture that oversees national forests and grasslands in the United States. Its website lists dozens of volunteer opportunities for young people, as well as in-depth information about forests and what foresters do.

Animal Curator

A curator is a person responsible for a collection. An animal curator is responsible for a collection of animals—usually within a zoo or aquarium, but also within an animal sanctuary, wildlife conservation center, or live animal exhibit. The curator is in charge of everything that involves or affects the animals under his or her care. Curators choose the animals within the exhibit, often acquiring them by trading with other zoos. They design exhibit space and make sure the animals get the right diet and veterinary care. They supervise animal keepers, veterinarians, and education and research staff. And they are key players in efforts to protect and conserve wildlife on the brink of extinction.

Zoos and similar institutions are critical to the survival of endangered species—many of which are so rare that their survival depends on captive breeding programs. The curator oversees these programs, making sure the animals have enough genetic diversity that the species as a whole stays healthy. Curators also oversee research studies, working with scientists who

At a Glance
Animal Curator

Minimum Educational Requirements
Bachelor's degree

Personal Qualities
Strong communication and management skills; passion for wildlife

Working Conditions
Offices, captive animal settings

Salary Range
As of May 2015, about $28,000 to $100,000, based on various sources

Number of Jobs
About 500 as of 2015

Employers
Zoos and aquariums, wildlife sanctuaries, animal exhibits

Future Job Outlook
No specifics are known

want to learn about captive species so that those in the wild can be better protected. And perhaps most importantly, curators work with educators to fulfill the primary goal of most zoos and aquariums—to teach the public about the animals with whom they share the planet. David Field, a former animal curator who currently directs both the London Zoo and the Whipsnade Zoo in Great Britain, is passionate about the role zoos play in conservation. As he wrote in an April 2016 blog post on the Zoological Society of London's website, "[Zoos] contribute research and data on animal ecology, physiology and behaviour; . . . develop ground-breaking veterinary techniques that are directly transferred to wild veterinary teams; and . . . have a unique ability to engage audiences, and inspire the conservationists of tomorrow."

In larger zoos and aquariums, curators often spend more time in the office than they would like on record-keeping and management tasks. But in smaller centers, animal curators often do it all. Rebecca Bose, curator of the Wolf Conservation Center in New York, interacts directly with the wolves and knows them all individually. She runs the captive breeding program at the center, which preserves two critically endangered species, the Mexican gray wolf and the red wolf—both of which were once completely extinct in the wild. Along with managing most of the center's programs, Bose is involved in caring for newborn wolves when the mother cannot, raising the center's ambassador wolves, administering veterinary care, and taking the center's traveling wolf to educational presentations in the community. Animal curators like Bose are able to experience the rare pleasure of working directly with the wildlife they strive to protect.

How Do You Become an Animal Curator?

Education and Experience

Animal curators must have a four-year degree in zoology, wildlife biology, or a related field. Curators at larger institutions must have advanced degrees, and many are experts in the animals they study. There are several routes one can take to become an animal curator.

An animal curator feeds a seven-day-old Mexican gray wolf pup—one of a critically endangered subspecies of gray wolf. Animal curators manage the care and health of endangered species and other animals in zoos, aquariums, and wildlife sanctuaries.

Some curators have spent many years as scientists studying animals in the wild. Others start as animal keepers or wildlife veterinary technicians and become experts in the animals they care for. Still others are experts in animal behavior and have worked as trainers in animal exhibitions.

Regardless of the route taken, all animal curators have spent their lives learning and interacting with animals. For instance, from a very young age, Geoff Hall, general curator of the Cleveland Metroparks Zoo, took every opportunity possible to learn about animals. He studied animals on his own as a child, he worked at a pet store as a young person just to get some experience in animal care, and in college he designed independent study courses so he could learn about the wild animals that interested him. He believes that all animal curators must have a commitment to lifelong learning.

Volunteer Work and Internships

To become an animal curator, volunteering is key. Volunteering is the way in which most people gain enough experience caring for animals to be hired into a paid position. Donating one's time and effort also shows that an applicant is passionate about animals—a key characteristic of an animal curator.

High school and college students can volunteer at their local zoo or aquarium, animal sanctuary, or conservation center. Some zoos and aquariums have junior keeper or junior curator programs designed for high school students, who help with animal care and educational events. Wildlife veterinary hospitals and wildlife rehabbers—people trained in caring for injured or orphaned wildlife—are always in need of volunteers. And while working with wild animals is usually preferable to working with domestic animals, helping out at a local animal shelter can also give a student valuable experience.

Volunteering also gives students an advantage when applying for an internship. An internship is usually an unpaid position that college students take to gain hands-on experience in their chosen field. Zoo and aquarium internships are very competitive, but in many cases, successfully completing an internship can help students secure paid positions after college.

Skills and Personality

First and foremost, animal curators love and respect the animals they care for. They are deeply concerned with conserving animal species and usually have a scientific interest in animal biology and behavior. The best curators are so passionate about wildlife that they do not mind working long hours, getting dirty, or doing anything necessary to benefit the animals under their care. However, curators must also be able to work well with people and have strong leadership and managerial skills. To do their jobs effectively, they need to be able to see the big picture and balance a variety of interests, such as animal welfare, public education, and the financial health of their institutions.

Curators must also deal with difficult issues, such making the decision about whether an animal should be euthanized. Working to preserve endangered species can also be frustrating—and sometimes it can be heartbreaking. For instance, some of the wolves under Bose's care that have been released into the wild have later been killed. Wolves are often killed because they threaten the livestock of nearby ranchers, and occasionally the same government programs that have reintroduced them into the wild will later choose to remove them by lethal means. "So much work, time, effort and resources go into saving these animals," Bose writes in an e-mail. "It's frustrating, to say the least, that we need to fight for their rightful place on this planet."

On the Job

Employers

Zoos and aquariums are most likely to employ animal curators, as are wildlife sanctuaries and conservation centers. Large animal exhibitions, such as SeaWorld and Disney's Animal Kingdom in Orlando, Florida, also employ animal curators.

There are probably fewer than 500 animal curators working in the United States. The Bureau of Labor Statistics (BLS) has not surveyed animal curators since 1998, when there were about 390 employed in the United States. As of 2015, there were about 2,400 animal exhibitions licensed by the US Department of Agriculture, of which only about 230 are accredited by the Association of Zoos and Aquariums (AZA). Accredited zoos and aquariums follow strict standards of animal care and welfare and are most likely to employ animal curators.

Working Conditions

Animal curators typically spend much of their days indoors in an office setting, as they must attend to record-keeping and other administrative duties. However, most do spend some time outdoors, overseeing the work of keepers and others who care for the animals and sometimes participating in this work. While they tend to maintain regular hours, a lot of work happens at zoos and aquariums during nights and weekends, and curators often oversee these activities. Travel is also involved, as curators often visit other institutions and take part in conferences and training events.

Earnings

According to the website Inside Jobs, the average pay range for an animal curator is about $28,000 to $86,000 per year. The AZA places the median salary for an animal curator at $51,280 per year. Salaries vary widely; smaller institutions and those in rural areas pay lower salaries, while large city zoos and aquariums pay higher salaries. Curators with the greatest managerial responsibilities earn the highest salaries, as do curators with advanced degrees, specialized skills, and many years of experience. A highly experienced animal curator can make $100,000 per year. For instance, the website Salary Genius lists the top zoo curator salary in California as $102,727.

Opportunities for Advancement

Animal curators tend to be at the top of their professions. In larger institutions, specialized curators (those which care for a group of animals such as primates or reptiles) can advance to the position of general curator, which oversees all animals in a collection. In a typical zoo, the only position above general curator is the zoo's director, an administrative position that many curators do not find appealing because there is little direct contact with the animals. Animal curators who want to advance may take a job with a larger institution. However, because this often means moving to a different city, curators tend to stay at a single institution for most of their careers.

What Is the Future Outlook for Animal Curators?

The BLS no longer tracks the employment of animal curators, and the growth rate in this profession is not known. However, after several high-profile animal deaths in zoos, more and more people have begun to question how ethical it is to keep wild animals in captivity, and some experts think that zoos and aquariums may be falling out of favor with the public. In addition, as scientists learn more about the physical and emotional needs of wild animals, they are realizing that, for some species, zoos cannot provide environments that meet those needs. For instance, the infant mortality rate for elephants in captivity is almost triple the rate it is in the wild. Because of this, some zoos are closing their elephant exhibits and moving their elephants to sanctuaries. Other zoos, aquariums, and animal exhibitions are ending their breeding programs and phasing out certain exhibits altogether. For example, the three SeaWorld parks in the United States have ended their orca-breeding programs and plan to eventually stop keeping the whales in captivity.

It is unclear if these trends will affect future job prospects for animal curators. Perhaps, in future decades, zoos and aquariums will be replaced by animal sanctuaries and conservation centers, and a curator's job will be more focused with species preservation and less on exhibition and ticket sales. One thing is certain—animal curators will always play an important role in protecting and preserving the endangered species on the planet.

Find Out More

Association of Zoos and Aquariums (AZA)
8403 Colesville Rd., Suite 710
Silver Spring, MD 20910
website: www.aza.org

The AZA is a nonprofit organization dedicated to the advancement of zoos and aquarium conservation efforts, education, science, and recreation. The AZA accredits zoos and aquariums, holding them to high standards of animal care. Its website includes information about wildlife conservation and a career center.

Conservation Breeding Specialist Group (CBSG)
12101 Johnny Cake Ridge Rd.
Apple Valley, MN 55124
website: www.cbsg.org

The CBSG's mission is to save threatened species by providing species conservation planning expertise to governments, zoos and aquariums, and other wildlife organizations. Its website includes a blog, a document library, and a news section.

International Zoo Educators Association (IZEA)
3605 E. Bougainvillea Ave.
Tampa, FL 33612
website: http://izea.net

The IZEA is dedicated to expanding the educational impact of zoos and aquariums by improving the education programs of its members. The IZEA works with zoo curators to develop programs that help animals thrive and people learn. Its website contains educational materials and a link to its journal.

World Association of Zoos and Aquariums (WAZA)
IUCN Conservation Centre
Rue Mauverney 28
CH-1196 Gland
Switzerland
website: www.waza.org

WAZA is dedicated to supporting zoos and other animal conservation centers in animal care and welfare, environmental education, and global conservation. Its website has information about conservation, industry news, and an online professional development center.

Environmental Engineer

What Does an Environmental Engineer Do?

Environmental engineers come up with practical ways to reduce the environmental impact humans have on the planet. Transportation, manufacturing, mining, agriculture, energy production—all of these human activities pollute the environment. While many other environmental conservation professionals study the effects of pollution on the environment or educate people about those effects, environmental engineers actually develop ways to prevent or reduce pollution at its source. They design technologies that reduce air and water contaminants, that dispose of waste products safely, and that clean up toxic spills. Some environmental engineers design smokestack scrubbers (devices that remove pollutants from exhaust), improve wastewater treatment plants, or develop better methods for cleaning up oil spills. Others develop technologies that make use of clean energy sources like solar and wind power. For instance, some recent inventions by environmental engineers include a clock that uses regular tap water as an energy source and an artificial leaf that converts water and sunlight into fuel.

Many environmental engineers work hand in hand with regulatory agencies. They monitor pollution levels and work with companies to bring their practices into compliance with environmental regulations. Some work with private companies to reduce their environmental impact, while others help to make sure new businesses use sustainable processes. They can also work with research scientists who study environmental problems like global warming or deforestation. On a typical day, an environmental engineer might complete a quality control check for a manufacturing plant, write an environmental investigation report for the government, advise a community about its concerns about water quality, collect samples in the field, calibrate equipment, or design new forms of technology in the lab.

Talented engineers have no problem making an excellent salary, and many have their choice of jobs and can live anywhere they wish (engineers educated in the United States are in high demand all over the world). Students who choose environmental engineering, however, usually want to use their talents to make the world a better place. Some put their degrees to work in developing nations that have contaminated water sources or dangerous levels of air pollution, while others address environmental problems in the industrial world. This is an excellent career for scientifically minded students who want to make a real difference on environmental issues.

How Do You Become an Environmental Engineer?

Education

For those who love science, math, design, and invention, pursuing a bachelor's degree in engineering is the first step to an exciting and fulfilling career in environmental conservation. While environmental engineering is becoming a popular major, graduates with any type of engineering degree can work on environmental issues. Choice of major should best match a student's area of interest; for instance, a student interested in sustainable construction practices might pursue a civil engineering degree with a concentration in environmental studies. An engineering degree can also lead to a wide variety of other careers, and it is not unusual for engineering majors to use their knowledge and training to become environmental lawyers, policy experts, research scientists, or the founders of nonprofits or green businesses.

Regardless of the engineering specialty, all engineering programs are competitive, and students must have a strong background in math and science to be accepted. High school students should take advanced courses in chemistry, biology, physics, and math. Students who dislike or have difficulty with these courses are wise to consider pursuing another area of environmental science—most experts agree that engineering is one of the most challenging college majors available.

Prospective students may want to apply to engineering programs that are accredited by the Accreditation Board for Engineering and Technology (ABET). Some employers prefer to hire engineers who have graduated from an ABET-accredited program, and attending such a program is necessary to become a licensed professional engineer—a requirement if an engineer wants to offer his or her services directly to the public.

Environmental engineering programs usually allow students to specialize in an area related to conservation, such as air or water quality, energy conservation, applied ecology, or engineering for developing communities. In addition to specialized courses, advanced courses in math and science are required, such as calculus, thermodynamics, organic chemistry, and microbiology. Students do lab and field work, and some programs require seniors to solve an engineering problem for a real-world client.

Many environmental engineers pursue master's degrees, and many colleges have combined undergraduate-graduate programs that allow students to earn a master's degree in five years. "An M.S. [master of science] degree is the best degree in environmental engineering," explained Christopher Corwin, an engineering professor at the University of Colorado, who was interviewed in August 2015 on the University of Colorado website. "Though it is generally not going to increase your starting salary greatly, it will give you the most professional mobility and be a short cut to meeting your career goals."

Volunteer Work and Internships

Internships—whether they are in an area of environmental engineering or another branch of engineering—are crucial to securing a good job after graduating from college. "Get internships," advised Corwin. "Many students go on to get their first full-time job with a company they started with as an intern. Even if that doesn't happen, it looks great on your resume and will give you experience in knowing what you are looking for in your first full-time position/employer." Many environmental engineering programs have arrangements with companies that need summer interns or offer internships to new graduates. Internships are also available through government organizations, such as the Environmental Protection Agency (EPA). For instance, one EPA internship involves helping to protect the water supply from mining activities. Interns monitor mining sites and develop plans to help mining companies comply with the law.

Many internships pay between $9 and $15 per hour, but unpaid internships with nonprofits are available as well. Many of these internships give students a chance to work on environmental issues, such as promoting clean air and water in developing countries. Regardless of whether it is paid or unpaid, internships give students valuable real-world experience in the field.

Skills and Personality

Engineers want to know how things work. They are often the kids who get in trouble for taking apart the toaster or the lawn mower. They love to solve problems, and they are curious and creative. They are also naturally good at math, which is important because they use math at work almost every day. While many people do not think of math having anything to do with creativity, advanced mathematics is often compared to the creative arts. Solving problems creatively with math and science is at the heart of what an engineer does.

Along with their creativity, engineers also have to be analytical and somewhat methodical when approaching problems—skills that many engineers learn in college. They also learn to work cooperatively on teams and collaborate with others, as well as how to communicate complex ideas to those who do not have an engineering background.

In addition to these traits, environmental engineers have a passion for environmental conservation. They usually love the outdoors and want to protect nature from the impact of human activity. As natural problem solvers, they want to change the physical processes that cause pollution and other environmental damage. Environmental engineers want to use their creativity to make the world a better place.

On the Job

Employers

Environmental engineers work for a wide variety of employers. Some work with engineering firms or consultant groups, while others work for architects, urban planners, utility companies, or manufacturing businesses. As of 2014, about 28 percent of all environmental engineers were employed by the government. Environmental engineers can also work independently as consultants, and many become entrepreneurs who start their own businesses.

Working Conditions

Environmental engineers can work indoors or outdoors depending upon their specialty. Those who work with architects or urban planners tend to work in offices. Those who work with environmental scientists or hazardous waste technicians tend to work outdoors. Extensive travel can be involved in this job, especially for consultants, who must travel to job sites, seminars, and conferences.

Most environmental engineers work regular business hours. However, when involved with a project, an environmental engineer may need to work nights and weekends to monitor progress or meet deadlines.

Earnings

The Bureau of Labor Statistics (BLS) states that the median income for environmental engineers in 2015 was $84,560, with a salary range of about $50,230 to $128,440 per year. According to the BLS, the highest earners worked for the federal government, with a median salary of $101,640 per year. However, the news magazine *U.S. News & World Report* claims that natural resources extraction industries (for instance, the oil industry) pay the highest salaries. Environmental engineers who work with nonprofits tend to earn the least.

Opportunities for Advancement

There are many opportunities for advancement in this field, especially for environmental engineers who pursue certifications and advanced degrees. To hold research and development roles or to teach, environmental engineers must have at least a master's degree. Holding a professional license also helps with career advancement. Continuing education is also crucial for all environmental engineers who want to advance; all engineers must continually learn about emerging technologies and the latest research in the field. Environmental engineers can also become board certified by the American Academy of Environmental Engineers and Scientists, a credential that demonstrates expertise and can improve job prospects.

As environmental engineers advance, they become supervisors or technical specialists in their areas of expertise. Some move into high-level management positions or become consultants, while others direct environmental programs or start environmental companies or nonprofits. Because of the flexibility of their degrees, environmental engineers are in a position to follow their interests and become leaders in almost all fields related to environmental conservation.

What Is the Future Outlook for Environmental Engineers?

The BLS projects that employment of environmental engineers will grow faster than average from 2014 to 2024 at a rate of about 12 percent. Crises in pollution levels and water contamination will drive a lot of this growth, especially as new energy processes such as fracking (removing natural gas from the earth) threatens underground water sources. As regulations increase, environmental engineers will be needed to help the government enforce those regulations, monitor pollution, and help businesses comply with the law. The BLS also expects many environmental engineers to retire in the coming years, creating opportunities for new graduates.

The employment outlook for female environmental engineers may be more positive than for their male counterparts. According to the National Science Foundation, only 33.8 percent of environmental engineers are women. While women are entering the field in greater numbers than they were in previous decades, many companies are also actively recruiting and hiring women—especially those with advanced degrees. This means that, for the foreseeable future, women entering the field of environmental engineering may have a slight advantage over men when applying for internships or looking for their first job.

For both men and women, however, the field of environmental engineering offers a wide variety of opportunities to make a real difference in conservation. Students who love solving technical problems will thrive in this career and will join other leaders in coming up with practical solutions to the world's conservation issues.

Find Out More

Accreditation Board for Engineering and Technology (ABET)
415 N. Charles St.
Baltimore, MD 21201
website: www.abet.org

ABET is the organization that accredits engineering program and ensures that accredited programs meet high standards of excellence. Its website contains information about accreditation criteria and a listing of ABET-accredited programs in environmental engineering.

American Academy of Environmental Engineers and Scientists (AAEES)
147 Old Solomons Island Rd., Suite 303
Annapolis, MD 21401
website: www.aaees.org

The AAEES is a nonprofit professional organization for environmental engineering and environmental science professionals. Its website has a wealth of resources, including an education and student center. Students are encouraged to become members.

Association of Environmental Engineering and Science Professors (AEESP)
1211 Connecticut Ave. NW, Suite 650
Washington, DC 20036
website: www.aeesp.org

The AEESP is a professional organization for educators in environmental sciences. Its website has resources for students, including a wiki site for students interested in becoming environmental engineers and a comprehensive list of links to colleges and universities in the United States that have environmental engineering programs.

National Society of Professional Engineers (NSPE)
1420 King St.
Alexandria, VA 22314
website: www.nspe.org

The NSPE is a nonprofit engineering association that supports professional engineers. Its website includes a jobs board, a news and publication section, and information and resources for engineering students.

Environmental Lobbyist

What Does an Environmental Lobbyist Do?

Many people have the mistaken belief that lobbyists are powerful insiders who bribe politicians with expensive gifts or make shady backroom deals to promote their clients' interests. In reality, lobbyists act as the voice of the people, educating lawmakers about the issues that their clients care about. They are experts in the fields they represent, and their job is to share that expertise with lawmakers. According to the "What Is Lobbying?" web page on the National Institute for Lobbying & Ethics' website, "Without lobbyists at all levels our government won't work. Lobbyists provide the most basic information legislators need and can't get. Lobbyists point out issues and areas of injustice that would otherwise go unaddressed. Lobbyists speak for those who haven't had a voice."

This is especially true of the work of environmental lobbyists. Environmental lobbyists

At a Glance

Environmental Lobbyist

Minimum Educational Requirements
Bachelor's degree

Personal Qualities
Excellent interpersonal and communication skills; determination

Registration
Required in most localities

Working Conditions
Offices; some travel required

Salary Range
As of 2015, about $20,000 to $110,000, according to various sources

Employers
Nonprofits; green businesses; political campaigns

Future Job Outlook
Positive, according to various sources

urge lawmakers to support policy that protects the environment. Many lawmakers have limited knowledge about conservation issues. In fact, without environmental lobbyists, it is possible that many environmental issues might never have come to the attention of lawmakers at all—at least not until it was too late.

Lobbyists who specialize in the environment and conservation are deeply concerned about the causes they fight for. They have expert knowledge about these issues, but they also have a thorough understanding of the legislative and political process. Over time, they develop a vast network of contacts within the political system—both with lawmakers who care about environmental issues and, perhaps more importantly, with those who might oppose environmental legislation. The job of an environmental lobbyist is to educate these lawmakers about what needs to change in the law and why. Most lawmakers rely on the lobbying industry to provide them with this information, as they usually do not have the funding or resources to do the research themselves. For this reason, a lobbyist's reputation for being truthful and accurate is very important.

An environmental lobbyist's job includes researching and analyzing studies, statistics, and other information pertaining to environmental issues; writing and distributing educational information; meeting with lawmakers and their staff; and giving presentations to congressional committees or legislative bodies. Through this process, they try to persuade lawmakers to vote for a piece of legislation that protects the environment—or against one that will harm it.

Sometimes, environmental lobbyists actually write new laws. For instance, a nonprofit might hire an environmental lobbyist to help it protect an old-growth forest. The environmental lobbyist would research the issue, draft legal language that incorporates the forest into a nearby national park, and then pass that language along to a member of Congress who supports this cause. Many lawmakers rely on lobbyists to provide them with this language—a first draft of a bill that will most likely be rewritten many times before it comes to a vote. The lobbyist will then work with the lawmaker and the nonprofit to try to get the law passed.

Environmental lobbyists can also do what is called "grassroots lobbying"—the process of educating members of the public and motivating them to urge their representatives to support an issue. To do this, they encourage the media to report on the issue, use the Internet to educate the public or contact voters, and help activist groups organize protests or educational campaigns. In addition, some environmental lobbyists work on the campaigns of political candidates who are sympathetic to environmental issues.

Because the general public has viewed lobbying as a somewhat sinister occupation in recent years, many lobbyists prefer to be known as political consultants, government affairs representatives, or policy advocates. Regardless of their title, most lobbyists must be registered with the federal government or with the state government in which they operate. Federal lobbyists and some state lobbyists must also disclose their financial records to establish that they are not using money or gifts to influence lawmakers.

How Do You Become an Environmental Lobbyist?

Education

An undergraduate degree is a requirement for this career, but the degree can be in virtually any subject. Most experts agree that a degree in political science, environmental science, or environmental policy tends to be the most useful. Environmental policy is a relatively new major. Students study ecology and the environment, as well as the laws and policies related to conservation issues. They also might study economics, statistics, and conservation issues like sources of pollution or methods to protect nonrenewable resources.

It is knowledge and experience that matters most in this profession. For this reason, students interested in this career should take every opportunity to educate themselves about the way government and politics work. They also should be experts in science and environmental issues. Most new graduates will need to demonstrate these skills—through internships, volunteer experiences, and performance at a related job—before they will be offered their first job as a lobbyist. Some experts estimate that new graduates must accumulate three to eight years of experience in political advocacy before they can become professional lobbyists.

Volunteer Work and Internships

In high school, students interested in a career in environmental lobbying should get experience both in government and environmental advocacy. Students can get involved in their school's student government or cover government matters in their school newspaper. Those who live near their state's capital should find out if it has a legislative page program. A page is a young person—usually of high school age—who volunteers to deliver correspondence and do other tasks for lawmakers. Page programs are an excellent way to learn how the government works firsthand.

High school students can also volunteer with environmental advocacy groups, which will give them an excellent idea of how lobbying works on the grassroots level. There may also be opportunities to sit in on state or local government committee meetings or hearings pertaining to environmental issues. It is a good idea to find a mentor who works in political advocacy. Mentors can open doors to experiences that would be difficult to gain access to otherwise, and they can help students get into the college program of their choice.

In college, students should seek out an internship in advocacy or policy work with groups such as lobbying firms, environmental advocacy groups, or political research organizations. Internships are important; lobbyists need a vast network of contacts and years of experience under their belts before they can become effective at their jobs, and internships are the first step to getting this experience.

Skills and Personality

Environmental lobbyists are extroverted people who enjoy networking and talking with others. They have good interpersonal skills and are excellent negotiators. They also are great communicators and are able to summarize complex issues for laypeople, both orally and in writing.

Environmental lobbyists are also persistent and determined. They are willing to work as hard as necessary to promote their cause and understand that results, not effort, are rewarded in this industry. They are also passionate environmentalists who want to make a difference.

On the Job

Employers

Environmental lobbyists usually work on behalf of nonprofit environmental conservation organizations such as the Nature Conservancy or the Sierra Club. They can also work for green businesses—businesses that have good environmental practices and want to strengthen environmental laws. Some of these lobbyists are employed by lobbying firms, while others work directly for nonprofits and businesses. Lobbyists can also work for public relations firms or for political campaigns. Because lobbyists work closely with legislators in federal and state governments, most are employed in and around Washington, DC, and state capitals.

Because not all lobbyists are registered, and because not all environmental lobbyists identify themselves as specializing in environmental issues, it is unclear how many environmental lobbyists are working in the United States. In 2016 there were 10,498 registered lobbyists working within the federal government. According to the Center for Responsive Politics, only 268 of those registered lobbyists advocated for environmental issues in 2016. However, this is just a fraction of the environmental lobbyists working today.

Earnings

It is difficult to determine an accurate salary range for environmental lobbyists. The Bureau of Labor Statistics (BLS) groups lobbyists with public relations specialists, who in 2015 earned a median income of $56,770, with a salary range of $31,690 to $110,080. However, the website Environmental Science groups environmental lobbyists with political scientists and estimates that environmental lobbyists make $102,000 per year on average. The career website Vault.com estimates that environmental lobbyists earn between $20,000 and $80,000 per year.

Working Conditions

Environmental lobbyists work in an office environment. They are frequently in meetings and often have to travel in order to consult with lawmakers and political staff members. While they tend to work regular hours, meetings can take place at night or on weekends, and they can work around the clock when an important legislative deadline is at hand. Environmental lobbyists also go to networking and social events as part of their job.

Opportunities for Advancement

Environmental lobbyists advance by developing their reputations. The more successes they have, the more in demand their services become. However, to be successful, they need to increase their expertise. To this end, many pursue advanced degrees in science or policy. Some also choose to work directly for powerful nonprofits or green businesses, but these opportunities are limited.

Many environmental lobbyists are not motivated by higher salaries—if they were, they would lobby for powerful groups like the oil industry or the financial sector. Instead, these professionals are motivated by their concern for the environment and the causes they fight for. Because of this, many accept lower salaries or even offer their services to nonprofits for free. They measure their success by the progress they make in protecting the environment. To the environmental lobbyist, advancement often means earning the opportunity to work the key issues that threaten the environment today.

What Is the Future Outlook for Environmental Lobbyists?

Most experts agree that there will be an increase in opportunities for environmental lobbyists through 2024, though there is not much agreement about how much growth this industry will experience. In 2012, the website Environmental Science projected a faster-than-average rate of growth of 21 percent in this field based on the fact that the Obama administration placed a great deal of emphasis on environmental issues in its political agenda.

The political climate will have a huge impact on the job prospects for environmental lobbyists. If the majority of state or federal lawmakers support environmental issues, nonprofits and green businesses will be more likely to hire lobbyists to help them pass bills that protect the environment. If a majority of lawmakers are resistant to legislation that protects the environment, nonprofits and green businesses will spend less money on environmental lobbying.

Regardless of the political climate, the pressing environmental concerns that threaten our planet will continue to get worse until laws are passed to address them. Issues like global warming, clean energy, and pollution will need champions in the political arena for the foreseeable future. Environmental lobbyists are those champions, and the work that they do will always be important.

Find Out More

American Association of Political Consultants (AAPC)
8400 Westpark Dr., 2nd Floor
McLean, VA 22102
website: http://theaapc.org

The AAPC is a professional organization of lobbyists, including environmental lobbyists. Its website includes a jobs board and a newsletter with industry news and strategy.

Environment America
294 Washington St., Suite 500
Boston, MA 02108
website: www.environmentamerica.org

Environment America is a group of research and advocacy organizations that works with a network of state-based lobbyists and advocates in order to make changes in environmental policy. Its website gives an overview of what a large and broad-based environmental lobbying group does to advance conservation issues.

National Association of State Lobbyists (NASL)
website: www.statelobbyists.org

The NASL is a network of state lobbyists and government affairs professionals who meet their ethical standards. Its website includes information about lobbying ethics and a list of member lobbyists operating in each state.

National Institute for Lobbying & Ethics (NILE)
3930 Walnut St., Suite 210
Fairfax, VA 22030
website: https://lobbyinginstitute.com

NILE is a professional organization for registered federal lobbyists. Its website gives a good overview of the lobbying profession as a whole: It contains in-depth essays that explain the value of lobbyists and the current status of the lobbying profession, a description of educational and certification opportunities for lobbyists, and a news section of current events and opinion pieces.

Pike Associates
203 Maryland Ave. NE
Washington, DC 20002
website: www.pikeassoc.com

Pike Associates is an environmental lobbying firm that advocates for the protection of the world's oceans and fisheries. Its website gives an overview of what an environmental lobbying firm does to advance specialized conservation issues.

Climate Scientist

What Does a Climate Scientist Do?

The majority of climate experts believe that global warming is the most potentially devastating environmental issue of modern times. Global warming occurs when excess greenhouse gases in the atmosphere trap too much of the sun's heat, causing polar ice to melt, sea levels to rise, and weather patterns to become erratic and extreme. Almost all scientists agree that human activity—specifically the burning of fossil fuels like oil and coal—is to blame for global warming. Environmentalists all over the globe are studying this issue to determine what can be done to avert it.

At the forefront of these efforts are climate scientists like Jean Jouzel, a Nobel Prize winner for his work on global warming. Jouzel has spent decades examining ancient ice in Antarctica for clues about how and why the climate has changed on earth over millions of years, and he uses what he has learned about the past to determine how to slow global warming in the present. "The

At a Glance

Climate Scientist

Minimum Educational Requirements
Master's degree

Personal Qualities
Strong analytical, critical-thinking, and communication skills

Working Conditions
Offices, labs, and outdoor sampling sites

Salary Range
As of May 2015, about $50,630 to $132,180

Number of Jobs
About 11,800 as of 2015

Employers
Government agencies, research and nonprofit institutions, universities

Future Job Outlook
Growth of 9 percent through 2024

scientific community agrees on a common message: it is not too late, but it is really urgent," he explained to journalist Fabiola Ortiz, who interviewed him in July of 2015 for the news website AlterNet. "If we want to keep the [average global increase in] temperature to 2°C [3.6°F] . . . we have to leave 80 percent of fossil fuels . . . where they are—that means, in the ground."

Climate scientists (also known as climatologists) like Jouzel use advanced math to analyze data and predict future climate trends. They must draw data from a large number of disciplines. Climate is affected by the sun, the wind, the gases in the atmosphere, the ocean currents, the plant and animal life on the planet, and of course, human activity. Also, to predict future climate, scientists must be able to reconstruct climate patterns in the past—long before there were any atmospheric records. To do this, specialized climate scientists known as paleoclimatologists use the fossil record, deep core samples of soil and ice, and a wealth of other information to reconstruct past climate conditions and identify trends in climate change. Most climate scientists are involved in research of major climate issues like global warming, but others research the ways in which the future climate will affect aspects of business or industry. These scientists advise businesses on issues such as the placement of a wind power facility, or whether the climate will affect a building site over the next several decades. Regardless of whether they are making predictions about the climate in a small region or of the entire planet, climate scientists are the experts when it comes to how human activity impacts the earth's climate.

How Do You Become a Climate Scientist?

Education

There are a variety of undergraduate disciplines that can lead to a study of climate. Future climate scientists can study physics, chemistry, geology, biology, engineering, or math. Some colleges have climatology programs within their geography departments, while others have atmospheric science programs within their environmental science departments. Students can also pursue an undergraduate degree in meteorology (the study of weather) and specialize in climate science in graduate school. Regardless of the degree program, students who want to work in climate science should take advanced math, statistics, and computer science classes so they can begin to understand data analysis and modeling.

Climate scientists need to have a master's degree or doctorate to do research, but those who only have a bachelor's degree can work as climate analysts or climate change analysts. These professionals usually interpret existing data and research for policy makers or businesses. They can also assist climate scientists with sample collection or data analysis. Some new graduates who plan to become climate scientists begin working as climate analysts while they pursue a master's or doctorate degree.

In graduate school, students focus on more specialized aspects of climate, such as atmospheric thermodynamics (the study of energy in the atmosphere), solar-terrestrial physics (the study of the way the sun affects the earth), and climate management theory. If possible, students should choose a graduate program that emphasizes the area of climate studies in which they are interested. In the last one or two years of a graduate program, students work on their own research project, which becomes their thesis (for a master's degree) or dissertation (for a doctorate degree).

Volunteer Work and Internships

While there is not much volunteer work available in climate science, there are internships available for both undergraduates and graduates. Interns can work for large companies that do climate research (such as energy companies), or they can work on research projects. An internship allows students to explore some of the career options available for climate scientists. Some internships pay well and are similar to full-time jobs.

Students in graduate school can also act as research assistants to climate scientists. Research assistants (also known as graduate assistants) hold the equivalent of internships within universities. These allow graduate students to work with established scientists on their research projects. Some graduate assistants also help professors run student labs, grade papers, and teach introductory courses. Universities often give research assistants tuition reimbursement and a small salary.

Students who have a passion for environmental issues may want to take an internship with an organization that fights global warming. These interns often help educate the public about the causes and effects of global warming or summarize existing research for lawmakers. These types of internships are useful for students who want to work for an environmental advocacy organization after graduation.

Skills and Personality

Climate scientists love math and sciences that use math (like chemistry and physics). Their love of math usually extends to computers, which can be programmed to make predictions based on an analysis of large amounts of data. Like all scientists, they are curious by nature, and they enjoy coming up with creative ways to use data and math to make predictions. Also, they like problem solving and the rigors of the scientific method, which ensures that predictions are based on facts, not on intuition or biased thinking.

Most climate scientists are concerned about global warming and how it will affect life on earth in the future. Those who are interested in activism must be excellent communicators so that they can communicate highly technical information to a nonscientific audience in a compelling way.

On the Job

Employers

Climate scientists work for the government, public and private agencies, and nonprofits concerned with environmental issues. Those who do research usually work for universities or research institutions, but they can also work for large companies, such as oil companies, that have concerns about how climate change may affect their businesses. Climate scientists can also work as consultants for environmental consulting, environmental education, or environmental lobbying firms.

Earnings

The Bureau of Labor Statistics (BLS) groups climate scientists with all atmospheric scientists, who had a median annual salary of $89,820 in 2015, with a salary range of about $50,630 to $132,180. Since climate scientists usually have advanced education, they tend to earn slightly higher-than-average salaries. According to the *Chronicle of Higher Education*, location of employment affects salary in the United States. In 2011 climate scientists working in Maryland made the most, averaging $112,470 per year, followed by New Jersey at just over $110,000 a year and Illinois at almost $104,000 a year. At the lower end of the spectrum, climate scientists in Connecticut made an average of only $61,180 per year.

Working Conditions

Depending upon their area of interest, climate scientists can work mainly indoors in the lab or outdoors in the field, collecting samples and atmospheric data. Those who work in the lab spend much of their time on the computer creating complex models to predict future climate conditions. If they work at a university, they may have some teaching duties, which include supervising the research of graduate students. Those who work in the field may join other scientists on research projects; they might drill into deep glacial ice in the Arctic, sample soil or measure volcanic activity, or take atmospheric readings at sea. Some climate scientists do a combination of lab work and fieldwork. Climate scientists who are employed by the government or for private companies usually work on projects that require them to take samples at a job site, do analysis in the lab, and write reports communicating their findings to laypersons.

Climate scientists usually work regular business hours unless their research projects involve travel, which can include round-the-clock work. There is a low risk of injury in this field, though proper safety precautions must be taken in the field.

Opportunities for Advancement

Climate scientists who do research can advance by earning a doctorate degree and publishing their research in academic journals. Climate scientists are usually paid through universities and research grants, and their salaries are based in part on their reputation with their peers in the academic community. For those who do research at universities, an important step in their career is getting tenure, which means that they cannot be fired except under due cause. Universities award their faculties tenure so they will feel free to do research without having to worry about how it will affect their jobs.

Climate scientists who work for the government or private industries can also advance by doing important research, but their salaries are usually based on the area of the country in which they work. In addition, private industry tends to pay more than government or advocacy work.

What Is the Future Outlook for Climate Scientists?

According to the BLS, employment of all atmospheric scientists is projected to grow by about 9 percent from 2014 to 2024, which is faster than average. While there are no growth projections for climate scientists, experts believe that opportunities within the private sector will be increasing as more people accept the reality of global warming. Many businesses employ atmospheric scientists to help them predict how the climate—or regulations pertaining to the climate—will affect their bottom line. Severe weather can disrupt shipments and deliveries, flooding can destroy infrastructure, and new regulations that curtail pollution can drive businesses to seek out alternative energy sources. In addition, governments are putting limits on the amount of carbon an industry can release into the atmosphere, and climate scientists who are experts in policy can help advise businesses on how this will affect them in the future.

Finally, climate scientists may be able to develop ways of reversing the effects of global warming. New technologies may be able to remove carbon from the air or stop it from being released in the first place. For this reason, there may be an increased demand in future decades for people who have expertise in climate science—both to understand the complexities of global warming and to help humanity reverse it.

Find Out More

American Association of State Climatologists (AASC)
website: www.stateclimate.org

The AASC advances the development of science-based climate services on a local and state level. Its website includes links to its publications and a list of educational resources available from its members.

Climate Institute
1400 Sixteenth St. NW, Suite 430
Washington, DC 20036
website: http://climate.org

The Climate Institute is an international organization dedicated to research on climate change and climate change policy. Its website has links to articles on climate change and the Institute's activities, as well as a list of internship opportunities for students.

Intergovernmental Panel on Climate Change (IPCC)
c/o World Meteorological Organization
7bis Avenue de la Paix
C.P. 2300
CH-1211 Geneva 2, Switzerland
website: www.ipcc.ch

The IPCC is the internationally accepted authority on climate change, providing objective information to world governments about climate change issues. Its website contains material from all scientific presentations by the IPCC, as well as information about the IPCC scholarship program.

Yale Program on Climate Change Communication
website: http://climatecommunication.yale.edu

The Yale Program on Climate Change Communication helps facilitate communication between the government, climate scientists, media organizations, and the public to further education about climate change. Its website has a wealth of information about climate change, including research, publications, and news articles.

Wildlife Veterinarian

What Does a Wildlife Veterinarian Do?

Wildlife veterinarians—also known as zoo veterinarians—diagnose and treat health problems in wild animals. They can work in a variety of settings; some care for captive animals in zoos and aquariums, while others work in the field, assisting scientists who study wild animals in their natural habitat. It is a career that allows students to combine an interest in veterinary medicine, a love of wildlife, and a passion for conservation issues.

Most wildlife vets do much more than treat illness and injury. For instance, according to Ellen Bronson, senior veterinarian at the Maryland Zoo, zoo medical programs focus mostly on preventative medicine. Vets like Dr. Bronson do routine health checks on each animal under their care, supervise births and monitor the health of newborns, and autopsy each animal when it dies. They monitor the animals' diets, groupings, environments, and anything else that might affect their health and well-being.

At a Glance
Wildlife Veterinarian

Minimum Educational Requirements
Doctor of Veterinary Medicine degree

Personal Qualities
Compassion; curiosity; problem-solving and decision-making skills

License
Required

Working Conditions
Clinics, labs, zoo and wilderness settings

Salary Range
As of May 2015, about $53,000 to $158,000

Number of Jobs
About 1,000 as of 2015

Future Job Outlook
Growth of 9 percent through 2024

A wildlife veterinarian examines a malnourished manatee calf rescued by fishermen who found it lying in the wild next to its dead mother. Like other veterinarians, wildlife vets diagnose and treat illness and handle routine health care. Some are also involved in wildlife research.

Wildlife vets also do research. In a March 2016 episode of the Maryland Zoo's podcast, Off Exhibit, Dr. Bronson explained, "There's so little known about zoo medicine. . . . It's a field that's really only been around for fifty years or so, so we know extremely little about a lot of our animals, and we learn all the time." For instance, the Maryland Zoo has a large exhibition of penguins and is therefore able to study them over time. Dr. Bronson and her colleagues pose questions about unknown aspects of the birds' health and physiology and then try to answer them by devising research studies. To share their knowledge, they publish their findings and share information at professional conferences. This work is crucial for the conservation of endangered species; the more that is known about wild animals, the more effectively they can be protected in the wild.

Wildlife veterinarians who work with animals in the wild often partner with scientists and work on research projects aimed at learning about a particular species behavior or physiology. They are responsible for handling the animal, performing health checks, attaching tracking devices, and monitoring the animal's health during data collection. Other wildlife vets are directly involved in conservation projects. For instance, Joe Smith took two weeks off from his duties as the director of animal programs at the Fort Wayne Children's Zoo to travel to the Mariana Islands in the Pacific to capture and relocate two species of endangered birds that are being threatened by nonnative snakes. Working with the Pacific Bird Conservation group, Dr. Smith acted as a veterinary consultant as volunteers captured about a hundred of the rare birds and moved them to a nearby snake-free island. Prior to release, he checked the birds for parasites, took blood samples, and fitted them with unique leg bands so that the population could be tracked. "Every species has inherent value," he explained in a May 2016 news article on the Fort Wayne Children's Zoo website. "We are all part of the same planet. Humans caused this ecological disruption, and it's up to us to fix it."

How Do You Become a Wildlife Veterinarian?

Education

Becoming a wildlife veterinarian is a big commitment. Students interested in this career should take as many math and science courses as possible in high school and get ready for more of the same—it takes ten to fifteen years of higher education and training to become a wildlife veterinarian. Many experts say it is just as challenging to become a vet as it is to become a medical doctor—or perhaps more so, because while human doctors study only one species on the planet, veterinarians study hundreds.

The first step is to get an undergraduate degree that emphasizes the biological sciences. Students should choose a degree program that will prepare them for veterinary school, which is a four-year graduate school comparable to medical school. Veterinary school is extremely competitive. There are only thirty accredited veterinary schools in the United States, and only six have exotic animal programs—schools that give students more experience studying nondomesticated animals.

Getting good grades and test scores is crucial to being accepted to veterinary school, and some schools require that grades be in the ninetieth percentile or better. Most undergraduates take their Graduate Record Examination and any additional required tests in their junior year and apply to vet school in the fall of their senior year. A letter of recommendation from one or more licensed veterinarians is usually required as part of the application, so it is a good idea to use internships and volunteer experiences to seek out professionals who are willing to act as mentors.

In veterinary school, students spend the first three years on classroom-based coursework. In their fourth year, they work in an animal hospital or clinic, rotating among different types of animals and veterinary specialties. In most vet schools today, students can choose a group of animals to study so they can best prepare for their future careers. This is not recommended for future wildlife veterinarians. Because they will be treating a wide range of animals, they should expose themselves to as many types of animals as possible. For instance, a veterinarian working in a zoo will draw on his or her study of cats to treat lions, horses to treat zebras, and cows to treat antelopes and giraffes.

After completing four years of study and passing the North American Veterinary Licensing Examination, new veterinarians will be licensed to practice veterinary medicine. For wildlife vets, however, there is much more to learn. Most complete at least one unpaid internship plus a three- to four-year residency program at a zoo or other facility that cares for wildlife. Internships and residencies are also competitive, and new veterinarians often study domestic animals or work in small animal clinics while they wait for a spot in their residency of choice. After completing their residencies, most will start working as wildlife veterinarians.

Volunteer Work and Internships

According to the Bureau of Labor Statistics (BLS), veterinary schools weigh an applicant's prior experience with animals heavily during the admission process. For this reason, students should start doing volunteer work with animals during high school. Even volunteer internships at zoos that are designed for high school students are extremely competitive, and prior experience working with a veterinarian or a wildlife rehabilitation specialist—or even working with farm animals or volunteering at the local animal shelter—makes a difference in whether a student is accepted.

In college, students should seek out more formal internships and volunteer opportunities to show their commitment to veterinary medicine and improve their chance of being accepted to vet school. These can be found at zoos and aquariums, at wildlife hospitals, and through animal conservation groups.

Skills and Personality

Wildlife veterinarians should be compassionate, curious, and ultimately driven by their love for wildlife and respect for the natural world. Since job duties are so varied, they should enjoy variety and be able to shift from doing research in the lab to wading ankle deep in animal dung at a moment's notice. Working in a zoo can be fast paced and stressful, and vets need to be able to tolerate the frustration of not always being able to diagnose or cure the animals they care about. Wildlife vets who work in the field must be patient and methodical enough to do research while at the same time being adventurous enough to handle wild animals in remote habitats.

On the Job

Employers

Wildlife veterinarians can work for a variety of employers. Many are employed by the government and assist conservation biologists who study endangered species and other wildlife. Some work with research scientists and are paid through research grants. Others work for zoos, aquariums, and large animal exhibitions. Still others work for wildlife hospitals, wildlife conservation centers, and animal sanctuaries. Highly experienced wildlife veterinarians also teach veterinary medicine and are on faculties at veterinary schools and veterinary teaching hospitals. Finally, some wildlife veterinarians have a private practice that treats domestic animals and volunteer their expertise to wildlife rehabilitators—trained volunteers who care for injured or orphaned wildlife.

Working Conditions

While most wildlife veterinarians spend at least part of their day in a hospital, lab, or other indoor setting, all of them get down and dirty with the animals eventually. Anesthetizing a wild animal for an exam is physically demanding and dangerous, even if the animal is in a captive environment like a zoo. Wildlife vets who do field research can spend weeks at a time living in some of the most remote places on earth, where they can be exposed to rare diseases, extreme weather, and other dangers. Regardless of where they work, all wildlife vets can expect to work long hours that sometimes include nights and weekends.

Earnings

According to the BLS, as of May 2015 the median salary for veterinarians of all specialties was $88,490, with a salary range of $53,210 to $158,260 per year. Wildlife veterinarians tend to make a lower salary than other veterinary specialists because they are paid by governments, grants, or nonprofits. The website Salary Genius places the average salary for all wildlife veterinarians at about $76,500, with a top salary of $108,000, but wildlife vets at the top of their field can earn more.

Opportunities for Advancement

Wildlife veterinarians never stop learning, and the more they learn, the more they can advance within their field. Those who have distinguished themselves among their peers have conducted extensive research, adding to the body of knowledge about wild species. They can also become certified in one or more veterinary specialties. As they accumulate knowledge about wild species, they become more valuable to employers. Those with the most experience earn the highest salaries.

However, most wildlife veterinarians are not motivated by money. They chose their specialty because they are passionate about the care and preservation of wildlife. For many, success means having the freedom and resources to design and run conservation projects, create zoo and wildlife medical centers, or conduct cutting-edge research on endangered species.

What Is the Future Outlook for Wildlife Veterinarians?

The BLS estimates that employment of all veterinarians is projected to grow about 9 percent from 2014 to 2024, a faster-than-average rate. Only a small percentage of graduating vets go on to specialize in wildlife; of the 78,300 vets working in the United States in 2014, only about a thousand of them belonged to the American Association of Zoo Veterinarians, and only 164 of those were board certified in zoological medicine in 2015. Because there are so few wildlife vets, and because concern about endangered species is increasing, growth in this specialized field may be faster than projected. The research wildlife vets do on endangered species is critical to their survival. For this reason, wildlife vets will play a crucial role in animal conservation efforts in the years to come.

Find Out More

American Association of Wildlife Veterinarians (AAWV)
1616 Piedmont Ave. NE, Apt. S5
Atlanta, GA 30324
website: www.aawv.net

The AAWV is a nonprofit group that supports veterinarians who specialize in treating free-roaming wildlife. Its website contains news for vets on topical wildlife issues, links to presentations, and a jobs board that includes internship opportunities.

American Association of Zoo Veterinarians (AAZV)
581705 White Oak Rd.
Yulee, FL 32097
website: www.aazv.org

The AAZV is a professional organization for zoo veterinarians and other zoo veterinary professionals. Its website contains a resources and education center that includes career information for students.

Association of American Veterinary Medical Colleges (AAVMC)
655 K St. NW, Suite 701
Washington, DC 20001
website: www.aavmc.org

The AAVMC coordinates the application process for all veterinary medical colleges in the United States. Students interested in becoming a wildlife vet can get advice and information about this career, as well as learn about the application process to veterinary school.

Tufts Wildlife Clinic
55 Willard St.
North Grafton, MA 01536
website: http://vet.tufts.edu/tufts-wildlife-clinic

The Tufts Wildlife Clinic is a part of Cummings Veterinary Medical Center at Tufts University. Its website describes the projects undertaken at the center and its most interesting cases. It also has links to volunteer opportunities for students.

Interview with an Animal Curator

Rebecca Bose is the curator of the Wolf Conservation Center (WCC), a private, nonprofit environmental education organization in South Salem, New York. Bose is currently working on a master's degree in zoology and is an experienced veterinary technician. She is also a member of the Species Survival Plan Management Group for both the red wolf and the Mexican gray wolf and oversees the center's captive breeding program. Bose answered questions about her career by e-mail.

Q: Why did you become an animal curator?

A: I have always had a deep passion for wildlife and veterinary medicine. Being the curator of the WCC enables me to feed both of those passions. I am able to make a difference in the lives of our captive ambassador wolves and critically endangered red and Mexican wolves as well as for wild wolves on the landscape. Being the curator here at the center allows me to have a direct positive impact on our animals and beyond.

Q: Can you describe your typical workday?

A: The beauty of my job is that no two days are alike. I have a unique position as I wear many hats here at the center. At larger institutions curators typically spend most of their time behind a desk. Here I am the curator, but I am also the keeper, the veterinary technician, the nutritionist, the volunteer coordinator, the enclosure design advisor, and so on.

A typical day can consist of the following: caring for the wolves (feeding, cleaning, changing waters), dealing with any veterinary issues that might arise, providing enrichment, procuring food (road-killed deer and assorted donating meats), handling Atka (our traveling wolf) on a program, walking Atka for our camp or after-school programming, capturing wolves for physicals, capturing pups for health checks, photographing the wolves for our website and outreach materials, and constantly monitoring the wolves via our remote cameras. I am in charge of overseeing any research that occurs at the WCC, so I often work with students and professors who are performing their research here. I am WCC's representative for both the Mexican and red wolf Species Survival Plans (SSPs), and I am on the management groups of both the red and Mexican SSPs. This means that I am constantly interacting with other cooperators who are involved in captive breeding programs for red and/or Mexican wolves. I spend a fair amount of time on the computer as well.

Q: What do you like most and least about your job?

A: I love that we are making a difference in the lives of the wolves under our care and providing them with the best possible captive lives (from habitat to diet). I also love that we are working to put wolves back on the landscape where they belong. I especially love when we take extreme measures in veterinary medicine to save a species from extinction (semen collection and banking, artificial insemination, etc.). For instance, when breeding females reach a non-reproductive age, we spay them and immediately put their ovaries on a plane to the St. Louis Zoo. There they extract the oocytes [immature egg cells] and freeze them for future use and research. This is just one example of the amazing lengths to which we go to save a critically endangered species.

Conversely, what I like least about my job is when the animals we work so hard to protect are killed in the wild. The politics that surround wolves make me sick. We seem to be fighting an uphill battle for what is right—coexistence with wild species—all the time. This often baffles me.

Q: What personal qualities do you find most valuable for this type of work?

A: When working with wolves it's imperative that you check your ego at the door. You must remember that it's not ever about you. You need to put the needs of the animals first, over yours, over your co-workers, even over the organization! I think you need be level headed, not overly emotional, and rational. Having so many animals under your care creates even more opportunities for sickness, problems, and death. You must always keep your cool and make decisions based on what is best for the animal as an individual and for the species as a whole.

Q: What advice do you have for students who might be interested in this career?

A: Experience! I think the best thing one can do is volunteer, learn, observe, and participate. Try to spend time at places like the Wolf Conservation Center. I think having a veterinary background is a plus. It gives you a better perspective on things. Schoolwork should ideally concentrate on biology or zoology, and I would recommend getting a bachelor's degree at minimum.

Other Jobs in Environmental Conservation

Biofuel manufacturer
Conservation activist
Ecologist
Environmental chemist
Environmental data engineer
Environmental geologist
Environmental lawyer
Environmental permitting
  manager
Environmental writer
Forest and conservation worker
Habitat restoration engineer
Hazardous waste removal
  specialist
Hydrologist
Marine biologist
Naturalist

Natural resource specialist
Park ranger
Professor of environmental
  studies
Recycling coordinator
Remediation project managers
Solar panel fabricator
Sustainability officer
Urban or regional planner
Water resources engineer
Water treatment plant operator
Wetland conservationist
Wildlife biologist
Wildlife protection coordinator
Wind farm developer
Zookeeper

Editor's Note: The US Department of Labor's Bureau of Labor Statistics provides information about hundreds of occupations. The agency's *Occupational Outlook Handbook* describes what these jobs entail, the work environment, education and skill requirements, pay, future outlook, and more. The *Occupational Outlook Handbook* may be accessed online at www.bls.gov/ooh.

Index

About the Author

Christine Wilcox writes fiction and nonfiction for young adults and adults. She has worked as an editor, an instructional designer, and a writing instructor. She lives in Richmond, Virginia, with her husband, David, and her son, Doug.

Picture Credits